Finding Drake's Feather

Courtney D Thomas

FINDING DRAKE'S FEATHER

Prelude

Saying goodbye is never easy, especially for young hearts. Grief can feel overwhelming, and it's important to acknowledge and validate those feelings. Finding Drake's Feather; is a story about a duck family who faces loss and learns to navigate the complex emotions that come with it.

This book is intended to be a gentle guide for children as they begin to understand the concept of grief. It offers a safe space to explore feelings of sadness, longing, and acceptance, while ultimately emphasizing the enduring power of love and hope.

I believe that by talking about loss in a sensitive and age-appropriate way, we can empower children to process their emotions, seek support from loved ones, and find healing in their memories.

Pictures shared throughout this story are real family photos used as dedication purposes in which this story was created.

I'm grateful I was in your life, and you were part of mine. Until we meet again, R.C.K.

Introduction

Have you ever felt sad because you missed someone who was gone? Maybe it was a pet, a grandparent, or a friend. This story is about little ducklings who miss their daddy very much.

This book is about the feelings that come after someone we love leaves us. It's okay to feel sad, to cry, and to miss them. We can talk about our feelings, remember the good times, and find ways to celebrate their lives.

Join the duck family as they learn how to cope with loss, how to find comfort in their memories, and how to continue living with love and hope.

1

PAPA DRAKES BIG SPLASH

The sun peeked through the branches, casting dappled light on the glistening pond. It was a perfect morning for a duck family. Mama Hen, her feathers a warm brown speckled with white, preened her sleek plumage, while Papa Drake, waddled around, his bright blue eyes sparkling with mischief. He was a proud father, with a chest puffed out with pride, and his quack was a joyful rumble that resonated across the pond. Three fluffy ducklings, their downy feathers as soft as clouds, were busy chasing each other around, their tiny yellow beaks chattering excitedly. Papa Drake would swoop down, his wings creating miniature whirlwinds as he playfully chased his ducklings, their delighted shrieks echoing across the water. He was a whirlwind of energy, always ready for a game of hide and seek amongst the reeds or a thrilling race across the shimmering surface. Mama Hen, a wise and patient mother, watched them with a gentle smile. She knew her ducklings were lucky to have Papa Drake as their father.

He was the heart of their family, a beacon of warmth and laughter that filled their lives with joy. Papa Drake, despite his playful nature, was a loving and devoted father, always there to protect his family, offering a comforting wing to rest upon, and showering them with endless affection. Their days were filled with endless fun. They'd paddle around the pond, weaving through lily pads, their tiny bodies dipping and bobbing with the gentle waves. Papa Drake would dive for juicy worms, emerging triumphantly with a wriggling prize, which he'd generously share with his ducklings. They'd preen each other's feathers, their gentle beaks carefully smoothing down every fluffy strand. Evenings were spent huddled together in their cozy nest, built high amongst the reeds, Mama Hen's soft quacks lulling her ducklings to sleep. Papa Drake, his body curled protectively around his family, would sing them soothing songs, his voice a warm melody that carried them into the realm of dreams. The ducklings, their tiny bodies nestled close to their parents, would drift off to sleep, filled with the warmth of their family's love, a love that felt as vast and boundless as the sky above. The duck family was a symphony of love, their laughter echoing across the pond, their gentle quacks weaving a tapestry of happiness. Papa Drake, their playful and loving father, was the conductor of this symphony, his presence a melody that brought joy and harmony to their world. They were content, a picture of perfect family bliss, oblivious to the shadows that were lurking just beyond the horizon, ready to change their world forever.

The pond was alive with activity. Mama Hen, her feathers gleaming like polished emeralds, led her ducklings in a joyful dance across the water. They were a blur of yellow fluff, paddling furiously, their tiny beaks chattering with excitement. Papa Drake as he was, affectionately known, was their undisputed leader, a majestic figure with a handsome black and white coat. He would dive and resurface, sending sparkling droplets flying, always keeping a watchful eye on his flock. Today was especially lively. Papa Drake had a new trick up his wing, a comical flip in the air that sent the ducklings into fits of giggles. They splashed and chase each other, their little bodies bobbing on the water. Mama Hen, her heart full of love, watched them with a smile. Life was perfect. The afternoon sun, warm and comforting, bathed the pond in a golden glow. Papa Drake, ever the playful one, decided to challenge his ducklings to a race. "Ready, set, go!" he quacked, diving into the water with a joyful splash. The ducklings, eager to impress their father, followed close behind, their tiny wings churning the water. Suddenly, the playful atmosphere was shattered by a deafening crack. The sound echoed across the pond, sharp and piercing, leaving a lingering silence in its wake. The ducklings froze, their joyous chatter replaced by a stunned silence. The sun, which had been shining brightly, seemed to dim, casting a shadow of fear over the pond. Mama Hen, her instincts screaming, immediately sprang into action. Her heart pounding with a mixture of fear and urgency, she scanned the water, searching for her beloved Papa Drake. But the pond, once so full of life, seemed empty, eerily silent. The ducklings, confused and scared, huddled close to their mother, their eyes wide with terror. One of them, a tiny yellow puffball named Pip, squeaked, "Where';s Papa Drake?", His voice trembled, carrying a note of fear. Mama Hen, her voice strained with emotion, tried to reassure him. "Don't worry, Pip," she said, forcing a smile."He'll be back soon." But deep inside, she knew something was terribly wrong.

The sound of the crack, the sudden silence, the absence of Papa Drake's familiar presence - all pointed to a chilling truth. Her heart ached with a growing dread, a sense of loss that threatened to consume her. She guided her ducklings towards their nest, her every movement a mixture of grace and urgency. The journey, which had once been a joyful dance, now felt heavy and uncertain. The ducklings, sensing their mother's distress, clung to her feathers, seeking solace in her warmth. The nest, once a haven of comfort and love, now felt empty and cold. Mama Hen, her eyes filled with tears, tried to hide her grief from her vulnerable ducklings. She knew they wouldn't understand, but her heart ached with a pain that was both profound and unbearable. She gathered her ducklings close to her, their soft, downy bodies offering a small comfort. She pressed them against her, her tears falling silently onto their feathers. She whispered words of reassurance, trying to convince herself, as much as her ducklings, that everything would be alright. But the truth was, she didn't know what to say. She didn't know how to explain the sudden absence of their father, the sudden void that had ripped through their lives. She didn't know how to tell them that the world, once filled with the joy of their father's presence, now felt cold and empty. The ducklings, sensing their mother's sadness, looked up at her with their big, trusting eyes. They chirped softly, their innocent questions echoing the fear that had gripped their little hearts."Mama," one of them asked, his voice trembling."Where's Papa Drake?" Mama Hen's heart sank. She knew this moment was inevitable, a moment she had dreaded, a moment she had hoped to postpone forever. But she knew she had to be strong, not just for herself, but for her ducklings, who needed her more than ever. She took a deep breath, trying to steady her voice. "Papa Drake," she said softly, her voice choked with emotion. "Papa Drake is gone." The ducklings, their little faces contorted with confusion and fear, stared at their mother in silence.

They didn't understand the meaning of the word "gone," but they could sense the sadness radiating from their mother. Mama Hen, her heart heavy with grief, felt the need to explain, to find the words to help her ducklings understand the profound loss they had suffered. She knew the words had to be simple, age- appropriate, words that could pierce through their innocent understanding, words that could bridge the gap between their confusion and her grief. She knew she had to explain the concept of death, the finality of it, the absence that it leaves behind. But she also knew she couldn't dwell on the darkness, the sorrow, the emptiness. She had to find a way to talk about Papa Drake's absence in a way that would bring them comfort, a way that would allow them to remember him with love and joy. She looked at her ducklings, their tiny faces etched with pain and confusion. She knew she had to find a way to help them understand, to find a way to make their loss bearable, to find a way to help them remember Papa Drake with love and joy. She gently stroked their feathers, her touch both reassuring and heartbreaking. She knew she had to find a way to help them through this, to find a way to help them heal, to find a way to help them find comfort in their memories. "Papa Drake," she said softly, her voice filled with both sadness and love."Papa Drake is gone, but he will always be in our hearts. He will always be with us." She paused, watching her ducklings, their little faces still filled with confusion. She needed to find a way to explain, a way to help them understand, a way to help them remember their father with love and joy.

She thought of all the happy moments they had shared, the playful games, the cozy evenings at the nest, the laughter that had echoed across the pond. She knew she had to share these memories, not just to remind them of their father's love, but to find a way to bring a spark of joy back into their lives."Remember," she said, her voice softening, "the time Papa Drake taught us how to fly? He would stand on the edge of the nest, his wings spread wide and encourage us to leap. He would say,"You can do it, little ones. You are stronger than you think." She could see their eyes light up, a flicker of joy replacing the sadness that had clouded them. They remembered, their tiny hearts filled with warmth and love. "And remember," she continued,"the time we all went for a swim together? Papa Drake would dive into the water, his body disappearing beneath the surface, and then he would resurface, sending sparkling droplets flying. He would say,"Come on, little ones. Join me for a swim." And we would follow him, splashing and laughing, our hearts overflowing with joy. She paused, letting the memory linger, letting the warmth of it seep into their hearts. She could see the sadness in their eyes diminishing, replaced by a faint glimmer of hope. "Papa Drake's love," she said, her voice filled with tenderness, "will always be with us. He will always be in our hearts. And we will always remember him."The ducklings huddled close to their mother, seeking solace in her embrace. They chirped softly, their little voices filled with a mixture of sadness and love.

They knew they would never forget their father; they knew they would always cherish his memory, they knew they would always feel his love. Mama Hen, her heart still heavy with grief, felt a small flicker of hope. She knew the journey ahead would be difficult, she knew the pain of their loss would linger, but she also knew that they would find strength in their love, in their memories, in their shared bond. They spent the rest of the evening huddling together at the nest, their silence filled with unspoken words of love and loss. They knew their life had changed, they knew their family was incomplete, but they also knew they had each other, and that was enough. Mama Hen waddled back to the nest; her heart heavy with a feeling of sorrow that felt like a giant stone in her chest. She gathered her ducklings close, their soft, downy feathers against her own providing a small measure of comfort. "Are you all right, Mama?"asked Pip, the smallest of the ducklings, his eyes wide with worry. "Yes, my dear," Mama Hen forced a smile, trying to sound cheerful, but the effort made her throat ache. She couldn't bring herself to tell them the truth, not yet. The truth about the loud crack, the sudden chaos, and the empty space where Papa Drake had been just moments before. She couldn't explain why her eyes felt hot and blurry, why her wings felt so heavy like they were filled with pebbles instead of feathers. She just wanted to hold her ducklings tight and keep them safe from the pain she felt inside. "It's just... sometimes, Mama Hens get a little sad," she finally said, her voice trembling a bit. "It's like a big, heavy feeling in your heart, a little like when you're missing someone you love very much." The ducklings looked at her with puzzled expressions. They didn't quite understand, but they sensed her sadness. They snuggled closer to Mama Hen, their small bodies offering a silent promise of comfort and support. "Papa Drake... is he missing us too?"asked Squeak, the most curious of the ducklings. "Oh, Squeak,"Mama Hen said, her voice softer now, filled with a yearning that she couldn't hide. "I think Papa Drake misses us very much too. He loved us all so much, and he would want us to be happy. He would want us to remember all the fun times we had together, and the silly things he used to do."

She remembered Papa Drake's playful dives, his funny little quacks, and the way he'd always make them laugh. She remembered the way he'd teach them to swim, gently guiding them with his strong wings, and how he'd always be there, waiting patiently for them to catch up"Remember when Papa Drake taught us how to play hide and seek?" she asked, trying to coax a smile from her ducklings. "He'd hide behind the reeds, and we'd have to quack and splash until we found him!"The ducklings giggled at the memory, their little faces brightening as they recalled the fun they had with their father. For a moment, the heavy feeling in Mama Hen's heart seemed to lift a little, replaced by a bittersweet warmth of love and happy memories. "He was the best Papa Drake in the whole pond," whispered Pip, his voice filled with love. Mama Hen nuzzled her ducklings, feeling a sense of comfort in their innocent love and shared memories. She knew that the pain would linger, but so would Papa Drake's love and their memories. They would find a way to live with the loss, to cherish their time together, and to find hope and happiness in each other's company. The ducklings huddled together, feeling the warmth of Mama Hen's embrace. They were still young, but they understood that sometimes things change, and sometimes people we love leave. They learned that sadness was okay, a natural part of life, and that love could still live on in their hearts, even though they couldn't see Papa Drake anymore. The sun began to set, casting a warm glow over the pond. As the shadows grew long, Mama Hen led her ducklings back to the nest, their little bodies trembling with the chill of the evening air. The nest felt empty without Papa Drake, the warmth of his presence absent. Mama Hen gently tucked her ducklings in, their soft chirps filling the quiet air. She kissed each one on the head, whispering words of love and comfort. "We'll be okay," she whispered, her voice laced with hope. "We'll remember Papa Drake and his love will always be with us." She looked up at the stars twinkling in the night sky, feeling a small flicker of hope ignite within her. Even though Papa Drake was gone, his love and memories would stay with them, a guiding light in the darkness.

They huddled together for warmth, finding solace in their shared grief and love. Mama Hen knew that this was just the beginning of their journey, a journey of healing, remembering, and learning to live with the absence of someone so dear. But she also knew that even in the face of loss, their love for each other, and their memories of Papa Drake, would continue to shine brightly. The ducklings, still confused and a little scared, gathered around Mama Hen, their tiny beaks trembling. "Where's Papa Drake?" Pip, the smallest duckling, asked, his voice barely a whisper. Mama Hen knelt down, her eyes filled with a sadness that even the young ducklings could sense. She gently stroked Pip's head with her wing, her voice soft and comforting. "Papa Drake is gone, my little ones," she said, her voice thick with emotion. "He's not coming back." The ducklings looked at each other, their eyes wide with fear and confusion. "Gone?" Quack, the most curious of the ducklings, asked, his voice filled with a sense of loss. "But where did he go?" Mama Hen drew a deep breath, her heart aching with the weight of her own grief. She knew this was a difficult concept for her ducklings to grasp, but she had to explain. "Papa Drake had to go on a long journey,"she said, her voice cracking slightly. "He's in a better place now." "A better place?" Waddle, the most playful of the ducklings, tilted his head, his little feathers ruffled."What's a better place? Can we go there too?"Mama Hen smiled sadly, hoping to ease their confusion."It's a place where there's no sadness, no pain," she explained, "a place where Papa Drake is happy and at peace." The ducklings were quiet, their little heads drooping in sadness. They missed their Papa Drake, the way he would dive into the pond and splash them with water, the way he would share his favorite juicy worms with them, and the way he would tuck them in at night, whispering stories of the stars. "But we still have Papa Drake's memories," Mama Hen said, her voice softening. "He's always with us in our hearts, in every laugh, every splash, every memory we share." She looked at her ducklings, their eyes filled with a mixture of sadness and confusion. "Remember when Papa Drake taught us to play hide-and-seek in the reeds?" she asked, a faint smile gracing her lips. "He would hide behind the tall grasses, and we would quack and waddle around until we finally found him, giggling with joy." The ducklings, even in their sadness, could feel a glimmer of happiness.

They remembered those moments, the laughter, the warmth of their Papa Drake's presence. Papa Drake might be gone, but his love and laughter still lingered in their hearts. They had memories, precious and bittersweet, that would forever remind them of their Papa Drake's love. "He loved us so much," Mama Hen said, her voice full of affection. "He was the best Papa Drake a duckling could ask for."She watched as her ducklings, nestled beside her, their tiny bodies huddled together for comfort. Even in their sadness, their love for each other, and the memories of Papa Drake, were their solace. He was gone, but he lived on in their hearts. "Papa Drake's love will always be with us,"she whispered, her voice filled with a quiet strength. "He'll always be a part of our hearts, no matter where he is." She gently nudged her ducklings closer, their little bodies pressing against hers."We'll be okay" she murmured, her voice filled with quiet reassurance. "We'll get through this together, just like Papa Drake taught us." The sunset painted the sky in hues of orange and pink, casting long shadows across the pond. Mama Hen, her feathers ruffled by the gentle breeze, gathered her ducklings close. They huddled together in their cozy nest, their little bodies pressed against each other for warmth and comfort. The pond, usually alive with the sound of Papa Drake's boisterous quacking and the joyful splashing of the ducklings, was unnaturally quiet. The silence was heavy, a palpable weight hanging in the air. It was a silence that spoke volumes of what was missing – their beloved Papa Drake. Mama Hen's heart ached. She missed Papa Drake terribly. He was the one who always knew how to make their days brighter, how to fill the pond with laughter.

She remembered his warm, comforting presence, his gentle quacks that seemed to soothe even the smallest anxieties. She looked at her ducklings, their tiny faces reflecting a mixture of confusion and sadness. They missed their Papa Drake too, their playful games with him echoing in their memories. "Where's Papa Drake?" chirped the smallest duckling, his voice barely a whisper. He looked up at Mama Hen, his eyes filled with a yearning that mirrored her own. Mama Hen swallowed hard, her throat tight with emotion. She didn't want to lie to her ducklings, but she also didn't want to burden them with the harsh truth of what had happened. "Papa Drake... he's gone," she said, her voice cracking. She reached out, her wing gently stroking the duckling's soft feathers,"He's gone to a place where he can swim in the biggest, most beautiful pond you've ever seen. A place where there are no hunters and no loud noises, just peace and quiet." The ducklings huddled closer, their tiny bodies trembling slightly. They didn't fully understand Mama Hen's words, but they sensed the deep sadness in her voice. "But he's still in our hearts,"Mama Hen continued, her voice softer now. "And his love will always be with us. We can remember him by playing his favorite games, by singing our favorite songs, and by sharing all the happy times we had with him. He wouldn't want us to be sad."The ducklings looked at each other, their little hearts heavy with the weight of their grief. They understood that their Papa Drake was gone, but they also understood that his love and memories would remain. The sun dipped lower in the sky, casting a warm glow over the pond. Mama Hen tucked her ducklings closer, their little bodies seeking comfort in each other. They were a family, bound by love, and that love would endure, even in the face of loss. They would remember Papa Drake, and his love would always be with them.

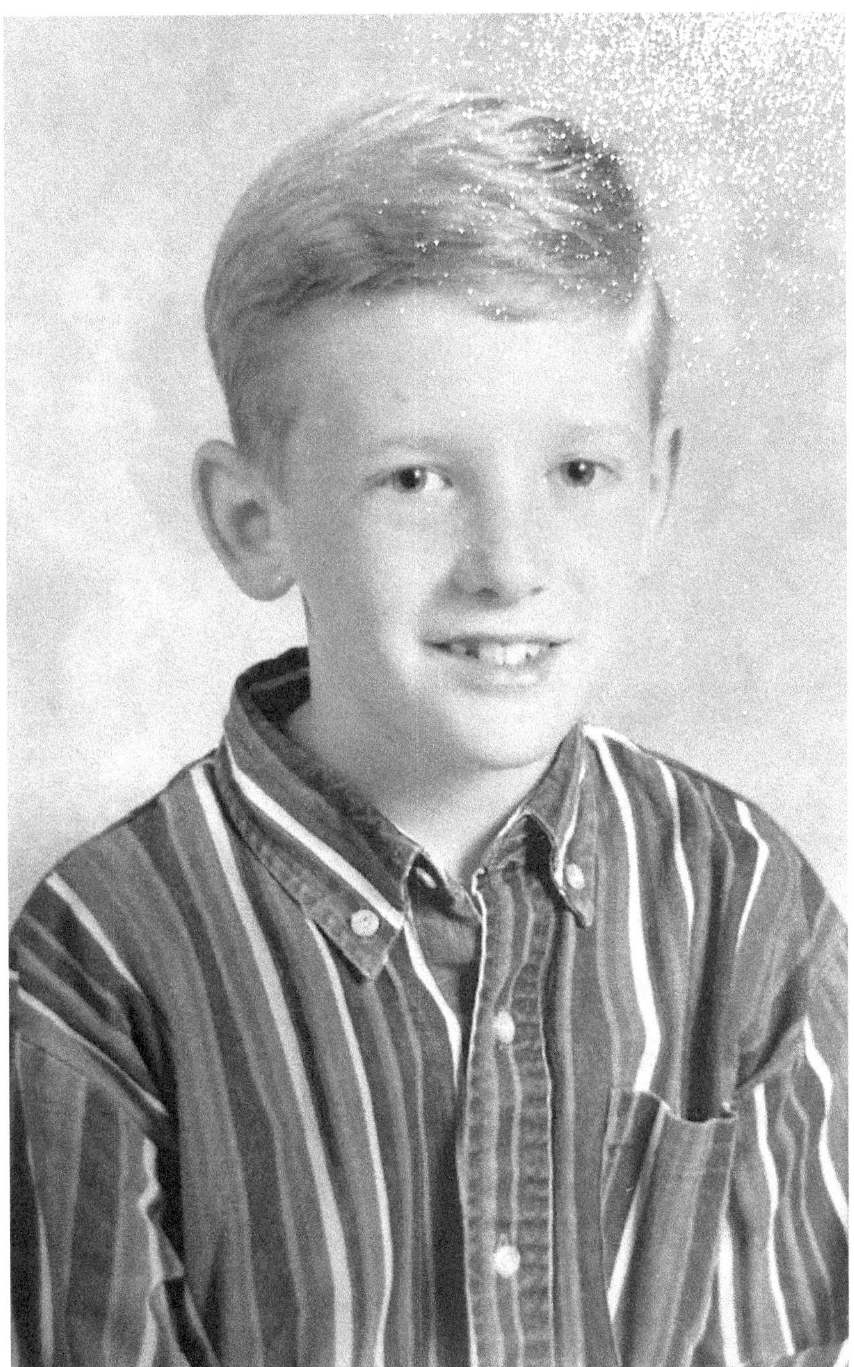

2

THE MISSING
FEATHER

The ducklings missed Papa Drake terribly. They missed his playful quacks, his gentle nudges, and the way he always knew how to make them laugh. They missed playing their favorite games with him, like "Chase the Bubbles"and "Hide and Seek in the Reeds."The pond seemed quiet and empty without him, and even the sun didn't feel as warm as it used to. One evening, as the ducklings huddled together near the nest, Mama Hen could see the sadness in their eyes. "I know you miss Papa Drake,"she said softly, her voice trembling a little. "But even though he's not here anymore, his love for you is still here. And we can keep his memory alive by doing the things he loved." The ducklings looked at her, their eyes wide with curiosity. "Like what?" asked one duckling, his voice small. "Like playing our games," Mama Hen answered, a small smile appearing on her face."Let's play 'Chase the Bubbles' like Papa Drake used to do."They all remembered Papa Drake's infectious laughter as he blew bubbles with his beak, each one sparkling like a tiny rainbow. Mama Hen blew a few bubbles, the tiny orbs floating gently on the still water. The ducklings giggled and chase after them, trying to catch them with their beaks.

The playful sound of their quacking filled the air, momentarily chasing away the sadness. Next, they played "Hide and Seek in the

Reeds."Mama Hen covered her eyes, counting slowly, "One, two, three... ten!"The ducklings scurried behind the tall reeds, their little bodies hidden from view. They peeked out from time to time, giggling as they tried to stay out of sight. It felt like Papa Drake was playing with them, his playful spirit filling the air. As they played, Mama Hen noticed one of her ducklings carrying a feather. It was a long, beautiful feather, with a soft, white tip and a dark brown shaft. It looked like a feather from Papa Drake. "Do you think this feather might be from Papa Drake?"asked the duckling, holding it out to his mother. Mama Hen gently took the feather, feeling the soft down on her fingers."It could be," she said, her voice soft. "It' a beautiful feather, just like Papa Drake." The duckling nodded, his eyes shining with a mixture of sadness and hope. The feather felt like a tangible reminder of Papa Drake, a piece of him that was still with them. It made them feel a little closer to him, even though he was gone."Remember when Papa Drake used to tell us stories about his adventures?" Mama Hen said, holding the feather close. "He was such a good storyteller, wasn't he?" The ducklings nodded eagerly, their memories of Papa Drake's stories coming back to them. He told them stories about his childhood, about his travels across the pond, and about all the other ducks he had met. His voice was always full of warmth and love, and he would often end his stories with a little wiggle and a playful quack. "He always told us that love never dies,"Mama Hen said, her voice filled with tenderness. "Even though he's not physically here with us, his love for you is still alive in your hearts." As the sun began to set, casting long shadows across the pond, the ducklings gathered around Mama Hen, their little bodies huddled close to hers.

They held the feather, a symbol of Papa Drake's love and presence in their hearts, even though he was gone. Mama Hen knew that the pain of loss would never completely disappear, but she also knew hat love and memories could help them heal. Papa Drake would always be with them, in their hearts and in their memories. They would carry his love with them, always remembering him with smiles and laughter. The ducklings were sad and missed playing with Papa Drake. They remembered how much fun they had playing tag with him, diving for pebbles at the bottom of the pond, and racing each other to the far bank. Mama Hen knew how much they missed their father. She wanted to help them feel better, so she gathered them around her."Let's play one of Papa Drake's favorite games,"she said, her voice soft and gentle. "That way, we can keep his memories alive in our hearts."The ducklings looked at each other. They weren't sure they wanted to play without Papa Drake, but they knew their mother was trying to help them. "Okay,"said one of the ducklings, a little hesitantly. "Let's play hide and seek." So, the ducklings hid behind reeds and water lilies, while Mama Hen counted to ten.

She laughed as she looked for them, pretending to be surprised when they peeked out from their hiding places. They all enjoyed the game, giggling and splashing around in the water. But even though they were trying to have fun, the ducklings couldn't shake the feeling of sadness. They missed Papa Drake's big splash in the water, his playful quacks, and his warm feathers. It was as if a part of their family was missing. As they were playing, one of the ducklings, a little yellow one named Pip, noticed something unusual. "Look!" he exclaimed, holding up a feather. It was a beautiful white feather, with a delicate pattern of black markings. Mama Hen saw the feather and her heart skipped a beat. "Oh, Pip," she said, taking the feather gently. "That feather might have belonged to Papa Drake."The ducklings gasped. Papa Drake's feather? It was a tangible reminder of him, something they could hold and touch. It felt soft and warm, as if Papa Drake's spirit was still with them. "It's like a little piece of him,"Mama Hen said, her voice filled with sadness and love. "Even though he's gone, he's still with us in our hearts and in our memories." The ducklings looked at the feather, their eyes filled with wonder and a little bit of sadness. They held it close to their chests, feeling connected to their father in a way they hadn't felt before. "We can keep this feather,"said one of the ducklings, "and remember Papa Drake whenever we see it."

Mama Hen nodded. "That's a wonderful idea," she said. "Papa Drake would love that." The ducklings held the feather, their small bodies huddled together, and they talked about Papa Drake.

They shared stories about his funny antics, his love for swimming, and his gentle care for them. Each story brought back a wave of happy memories, but also a pang of longing for their father. As they talked, Mama Hen noticed that the ducklings were starting to feel a little better. They were still sad, but they were also starting to remember all the good times they had with Papa Drake. They realized that his love and spirit lived on, even though he was no longer physically present. "We should find a special place for the feather,"aid one of the ducklings. "A place where we can always remember Papa Drake and share stories about him."Mama Hen smiled. "That's a wonderful idea," she said. "Let's find a special spot by the pond where we can create a little memorial for him." Together, the ducklings and Mama Hen found a quiet spot by the edge of the pond, where the water lilies grew thick and the willows swayed gently in the breeze. They gathered some pebbles and twigs and built a small pile, creating a place where they could lay Papa Drake's feather and remember him. "This will be our special place for Papa Drake," said Mama Hen. "We can come here whenever we want to remember him and share stories about his love for us." The ducklings nodded in agreement. They carefully placed Papa Drake's feather on top of the small pile, and then they huddled together, their bodies warming each other. They felt a sense of comfort and peace in their shared grief and their love for their father. "He's always with us,"said one of the ducklings, looking up at the sky. "Yes," said Mama Hen, her voice soft and gentle. "He's always with us, in our hearts and in our memories." The feather became a symbol of Papa Drake's love and presence in their hearts, even though he was gone. They held onto it, feeling his warmth and his love, and they knew that they would never forget him. Mama Hen gathered her ducklings close, their small bodies huddled against hers. They were all sitting on a smooth, flat rock by the edge of the pond, the water lapping gently against the shore. "Remember the time Papa Drake took us all on a grand adventure?" she asked, her voice a soft murmur.

The ducklings exchanged glances, their eyes reflecting a mix of sadness and curiosity. They missed their Papa Drake Duck dearly, and they longed to hear stories about him. "He took us all the way to the other side of the pond!"Mama Hen continued, her voice full of warmth. "We swam through the reeds, dodging water lilies and playful fish. He even showed us a secret spot where the water was crystal clear, and we could see all the colorful pebbles at the bottom." One of the ducklings, a small, fluffy creature named Pip, chirped up. "Do you remember, Mama Hen? Papa Drake taught us to dive for the shiny pebbles?"Mama Hen chuckled. "Oh, yes! You were so proud of yourself, Pip, when you finally managed to grab a pebble with your beak. You were so excited, you almost flew out of the water!"The other ducklings giggled, remembering the incident. Papa Drake had been so proud of them, cheering them on with his deep, rumbling voice. Their Papa Drake had always been the biggest cheerleader, encouraging them to be brave and try new things. "And remember the day Papa Drake taught us to fly?" Mama Hen asked, her voice filled with nostalgia. "He would stand on the edge of the nest, flapping his strong wings, and he'd encourage us to jump. At first, we were scared, but he kept saying, "You can do it! Just trust your wings!" Another duckling, a playful little fellow named Quack, chimed in, "I remember! I was so nervous at first, but then Papa Drake gave me a little nudge, and I flew! It felt amazing!" The ducklings, remembering their first clumsy attempts at flight, shared stories of their adventures. Papa Drake had been patient and supportive, never letting them get discouraged. He had taught them how to use their wings, how to soar through the sky, how to feel the wind beneath their feathers. "Papa Drake loved to watch us fly," Mama Hen said, a gentle smile touching her beak. "He'd fly alongside us, his big wings creating a gentle breeze that would lift us higher and higher. He was always so proud of us."

The ducklings sat in silence for a while, their thoughts drifting back to those happy moments with Papa Drake. They missed his warm presence, his booming laughter, his gentle encouragement. But they also realized that his love and his memories lived on in their hearts. "Papa Drake was the best duck in the whole world,"Mama Hen whispered, her voice filled with love. "He loved us more than anything. And even though he's not with us anymore, we can still feel his love, and we can still remember all the wonderful things he taught us."The ducklings nodded, their eyes filled with tears. They knew that Papa Drake was gone, but his love and memories were a treasure that they would always cherish. Mama Hen, sensing their sadness, nudged them closer to her. "We'll always remember Papa Drake," she said, her voice firm and reassuring. "And we'll always carry his love in our hearts." She looked out over the pond, its surface shimmering in the afternoon sun. "Papa Drake would want us to be happy," she said. "He would want us to keep exploring, keep learning, keep loving each other. He would want us to live life to the fullest, just like he did." The ducklings, comforted by Mama Hen's words, began to share more stories about Papa Drake. They remembered his playful antics, his gentle wisdom, and his unwavering love for them. They realized that even though their Papa Drake was gone, his spirit lived on in their hearts. As the sun began to set, casting long shadows across the pond, Mama Hen led her ducklings towards their nest. They walked slowly, their small bodies huddled together for warmth and comfort. They carried the memory of Papa Drake with them, his love a beacon guiding them through the darkness. The ducklings missed playing with Papa Drake.

They would have played their favorite games all day long if he were there. He was always so good at making them laugh. Mama Hen noticed their sadness and said, "I know you miss Papa Drake very much, my little ones. Why don't we play some of his favorite games with him in our hearts? We can keep his memory alive through our games." They all agreed, and Mama Hen led them in a game of hide-and-seek. They giggled as they hid behind the reeds and rocks, pretending Papa Drake was the one searching for them. They played with their beaks, dipping them into the water, pretending to be Papa Drake's playful friend. As they played, one of the ducklings, a tiny duckling named Pip, discovered a feather. It was a bright blue feather, shimmering in the sunlight. Pip picked it up and carefully examined it. "Mama Hen, do you think this could be Papa Drake's feather?" Pip asked, his tiny voice filled with wonder. Mama Hen looked at the feather, her eyes soft. "It might be, Pip. Papa Drake's feathers were just as blue and beautiful as this one. He loved to preen his feathers and make them look their best." "He always said his feathers were his armor," another duckling, named Dot, added, remembering Papa Drake's words. "He said they helped him keep us safe." Mama Hen smiled softly. "That's right, Dot. Papa Drake was a strong and brave duck, always protecting his family.

He loved all of you so much." The ducklings felt their hearts grow warm with these memories of their father. They shared their stories of Papa Drake, remembering his playful antics, his funny quack, and the way he always made them feel safe and loved. "We should have a special place to remember Papa Drake," Pip suggested, looking around at the beautiful pond. "A place where we can share stories about him and keep his memory alive," Dot agreed. Mama Hen, who had been listening to their conversation, felt a lump in her throat. She knew how much the ducklings missed Papa Drake, and she wanted them to have a place where they could grieve and heal. "That's a wonderful idea, my ducklings," Mama Hen said, her voice full of warmth. "Let's find a special spot by the pond where we can remember Papa Drake together." They walked around the pond, searching for the perfect place. They wanted a spot that was peaceful and quiet, where they could feel close to Papa Drake's spirit. Finally, they found it - a small clearing by the pond, surrounded by tall reeds and willow trees. The sun dappled through the leaves, creating a beautiful mosaic of light and shadow on the ground. "This is it," Pip said, his eyes shining with joy. "This is our place for Papa Drake." The ducklings gathered in the clearing, their small bodies huddled close together. They held onto the feather, a tangible reminder of Papa Drake's love and presence in their hearts.

It was a symbol of their strength and resilience, a reminder that even though Papa Drake was gone, his love would always be with them. They started sharing their memories of Papa Drake, their voices filled with both sadness and love. Mama Hen joined them, sharing her own stories of her beloved husband. She told them about how Papa Drake used to wake her up with his soft quacks, how he would catch the juiciest worms for her, and how he would always make her laugh. As the ducklings shared their stories, they realized that Papa Drake was more than just a father, a husband, or a duck. He was a part of them, woven into the fabric of their lives. They carried his love and his spirit within their hearts, and they knew that he would always be with them, in every ripple on the pond, in every rustle of the reeds, in every whisper of the wind. The clearing became their place of healing, a sanctuary where they could feel close to Papa Drake, share their grief, and find comfort in each other's love. They would often visit the clearing, sitting in the dappled sunlight, remembering their father and sharing their stories. As the days turned into weeks, the ducklings started to heal. They still missed Papa Drake dearly, but they also realized that life went on. They learned to find joy in new experiences, like learning to fly and exploring the vast expanse of the pond.

They discovered new friends among the other ducklings, and they learned to laugh again. The feather, which they kept tucked safely in their nest, became a symbol of Papa Drake's enduring love. It reminded them that even though their father was gone, his love was still present in their lives. It was a reminder that love, like a feather, could soar above the pain of loss and carry them through the darkest of times. The clearing by the pond became a sacred place, a testament to their love for Papa Drake and a symbol of their resilience. They knew that they would never forget their father, and his memory would always be a part of their lives. They would forever cherish their memories of Papa Drake, and they would always remember the special place where they shared their stories, found comfort, and learned to heal The ducklings, now filled with a mix of sadness and newfound determination, waddled towards the pond, their tiny webbed feet pattering softly against the soft earth. Mama Hen, her eyes glistening with unshed tears, watched them with a heavy heart. She knew they were struggling to understand their loss, and she longed to shield them from the pain that gnawed at her own soul. But she knew that hiding the truth wouldn't help. Instead, she had decided to embrace their grief, to face it together as a family. "Remember how much Papa Drake loved playing hide-and- seek?" Mama Hen asked softly, her voice wavering with emotion. "Let's play a game to keep his memory alive."The ducklings, their eyes still red and puffy from crying, nodded slowly. Their hearts ached with the absence of Papa Drake, their playful father. But the thought of playing his favorite games sparked a flicker of hope in their weary spirits.

They started with their classic game of "Duck, Duck, Goose." As they waddled in a circle, Mama Hen called out "Duck"and "Goose" with a feigned cheerfulness, trying to keep their spirits high. The ducklings, however, found it hard to laugh. Their giggles were choked with sadness, their voices barely a whisper. As the game continued, one of the ducklings stumbled upon something in the grass. It was a feather, soft and brown, with delicate barbs that tickled their tiny beak. "Look, Mama!"chirped the duckling, its eyes widening in surprise. "A feather!"Mama Hen knelt down, her heart swelling with a bittersweet mixture of pain and hope. "That feather," she said, her voice trembling slightly, "might have belonged to your father. He was a very proud duck, always taking care of his beautiful feathers." The ducklings huddled together, their tiny wings trembling with a mixture of sadness and wonder. They carefully examined the feather, its velvety texture soft against their beaks. It felt like a piece of Papa Drake, a tangible reminder of his presence in their lives. Mama Hen continued, her voice now softer and more gentle. "Papa Drake loved you all very much. He was always so proud of his little ducklings, and he would often tell me stories about each of you. He would laugh and say, "My little ducklings are the best in the whole pond!"The ducklings listened intently, their little heads cocked to one side as if trying to remember the sounds of their father's voice, his hearty laughter echoing in their memories. They recalled his playful antics, his gentle nudges, his warm embrace.

"Remember that time Papa Drake took us all on a grand adventure to the willow tree?" one of

the ducklings asked, his voice barely a whisper. "We had so much fun!" Mama Hen smiled sadly, her eyes filled with tears. "Oh yes," she said, her voice choked with emotion. "He was such a wonderful father. Always full of surprises and adventure." The ducklings, their hearts filled with a mix of sadness and fond memories, decided to create a special place to remember their father. They carefully collected twigs and leaves, creating a small mound near the edge of the pond. "We'll call it Papa Drake's Corner,"suggested one of the ducklings, his voice barely above a whisper. Mama Hen nodded in agreement. "A place where we can remember his love and his adventures, and share all the stories about him." As the sun began to set, painting the sky in hues of orange and purple, the ducklings gathered around Papa Drake's Corner, holding the feather close to their hearts. It was a symbol of Papa Drake's love, a reminder of his presence even in his absence. The ducklings knew that life would never be the same without Papa Drake, but they also knew that his love would forever guide them. They had his feather, a tangible reminder of his love, and their memories, a treasure trove of joy and laughter that would always warm their hearts. And so, the ducklings, huddled together in their nest, their tiny hearts heavy with grief, found comfort in their shared memories, in the feather that whispered tales of Papa Drake's love, and in the hope that his spirit would forever be with them.

3

―――――――

NEW FRIENDS AND LAUGHTER

One day, as the ducklings were splashing around in the shallows, Mama Hen noticed a group of ducks huddled together on the other side of the pond. They were a family, just like theirs, with a Mama Hen and several ducklings. The ducklings, still sad and shy from missing Papa Drake, watched the new family with a mixture of curiosity and apprehension. "Look, Mama Hen,"whispered one duckling, pointing a tiny wing. "They're playing!" The new ducklings were chasing each other around a clump of reeds, their cheerful quacks echoing across the pond. They looked so carefree, so happy, that the ducklings couldn't help but feel a pang of longing. "They're just like us," said another duckling, his voice tinged with sadness. "They have their own Papa Drake, don't they?" Mama Hen saw the longing in her ducklings eyes and knew they were missing Papa Drake even more. She gently stroked their downy feathers with her wing, whispering, "Yes, they do, but that doesn't mean they are any less special or loved. We all deserve friends, even when we are sad." The ducklings looked at Mama Hen, their eyes wide and curious. She continued, "Remember how much Papa Drake loved making new friends? He always said that having friends makes life more fun and exciting." The ducklings pondered this, remembering the times Papa Drake had introduced them to other ducks, birds, and even a curious little frog.

29

They realized that their Papa Drake would want them to be happy and make new friends, even if he wasn't there to introduce them. Mama Hen encouraged her ducklings to swim closer to the new family. "Let's go say hello,"she said, her voice warm and inviting. "Maybe we can play together."The ducklings, hesitant at first, slowly paddled towards the new family. They held their heads low, unsure of how they would be received. The new Mama Hen, noticing the timid ducklings, swam towards them with a friendly smile. "Hello there!" she chirped, her voice gentle and kind. "My name is Willow. What are your names?" The ducklings, reassured by Willow's friendly demeanor, introduced themselves one by one. Willow, in turn, introduced her own ducklings, each with a name as unique and colorful as their feathers. "It's nice to meet you all,"said Willow, extending her wing in a gesture of welcome."My ducklings have been wanting to make new friends. Why don't you all play together?"The new ducklings, eager to make friends, chirped excitedly and swam towards the ducklings. They started to play a game of tag, chasing each other around the pond with joyous squeals. The ducklings, slowly overcoming their initial fear and sadness, joined in the laughter and fun. As the day wore on, the two families spent time together, sharing stories, playing games, and swimming in the sun.

The new ducklings, playful and energetic, brought a new vibrancy to the ducklings lives. The ducklings, in turn, shared their stories about Papa Drake with their new friends. They talked about his silly games, his love for swimming, and his kind and gentle nature. The new ducklings listened intently, their eyes reflecting a mix of empathy and understanding. They too had lost their Papa Drake long ago, and they understood the pain of missing someone dearly. Sharing their stories and grief with each other, the ducklings felt a sense of comfort and acceptance. They realized that even though they were different, they all shared a common bond of love, loss, and healing. Willow, watching her ducklings and the ducklings play together, felt a wave of happiness wash over her. She knew that Papa Drake would have been proud of them for reaching out to each other and finding friendship in the midst of their sorrow. As the sun began to set, casting long shadows across the pond, the two families gathered together, their hearts filled with a newfound warmth and camaraderie. The ducklings, their eyes sparkling with joy, realized that Papa Drake's legacy of love and kindness lived on in their hearts and in their newfound friendship. They had learned that even though they missed Papa Drake dearly, they could still find happiness and make new connections. They had found a new family, a new source of joy, and a new chapter in their lives, all thanks to the kindness of a Mama Hen named Willow and the spirit of their beloved Papa Drake. At first, the new ducklings seemed like a blur of feathers and quacks. The little ones huddled close to Mama Hen, unsure if they wanted to play with these unfamiliar faces. They remembered how much fun they used to have with Papa Drake, and nothing felt quite the same without him. The new ducklings, sensing their hesitation, stayed a little distance away. Mama Hen, noticing their fear, gently nudged them towards the new arrivals. "Come on, my little ones," she said, her voice soft but encouraging. "It's okay to be scared.

But remember, Papa Drake would want you to be happy. And these little ducks are here to play too." One of the new ducklings, a tiny yellow one with a bright orange beak, cautiously waddled forward. He tilted his head, looking at the familiar ducklings with wide, curious eyes. He seemed to be asking, "Can I play too?" The little ones, seeing his kind face and gentle eyes, felt a little braver. One of them, a fluffy brown duckling with a mischievous twinkle in his eye, took a step forward. "What's your name?" he asked. "I'm Sunny,"the yellow duckling answered, his beak curving into a smile. "I'm Rusty," the brown duckling replied, his tail feathers wiggling with excitement. "Do you want to play hide-and-seek with us?" Sunny's eyes lit up. "Hide-and-seek? I love hide-and-seek!" And with that, the ice was broken. The ducklings, their fear slowly fading, began to play with their new friends. They splashed and chased each other in the pond, their laughter echoing across the water. As they played, they felt a glimmer of joy return to their hearts. The games were different from the ones they used to play with Papa Drake. But there was a new kind of joy in these games, a joy born of shared laughter and friendship. Sunny, with his playful energy, reminded them of Papa Drake's mischievous spirit. Rusty, with his adventurous spirit, reminded them of the fun they used to have together. One afternoon, as they were playing tag by the reeds, one of the ducklings stumbled upon a small, smooth stone. He picked it up, examining it curiously. "Look!"he cried, holding it out to the others. "It's a beautiful stone! It reminds me of Papa Drake."The other ducklings gathered around, their eyes filled with curiosity. "Really?"Sunny asked. "How does it remind you of Papa Drake?""I don't know," the duckling replied, his voice soft.

"It just feels like him. Like he's here with us." The other ducklings nodded, their hearts filled with a mix of sadness and warmth. They knew that Papa Drake was gone, but they also knew that his love and memories lived on in their hearts. The stone, a simple gift from nature, felt like a tangible reminder of him. As the sun began to set, casting long shadows across the pond, the ducklings gathered by the special place they had made for Papa Drake. They shared stories about him, remembering his playful antics, his comforting presence, and his endless love. "He loved to chase butterflies," one duckling said, a smile tugging at his beak. "He used to sing us lullabies," another added, his voice filled with nostalgia. "He always knew how to make us laugh,"a third duckling chirped. As they shared their stories, the ducklings felt a sense of peace wash over them. They realized that even though Papa Drake was gone, his love and memories were still alive in their hearts. They could remember him, cherish him, and carry his love with them forever. The new ducklings, listening intently, were touched by the stories. They felt a connection to Papa Drake, even though they never met him. They understood that these were special memories, ones that were worth cherishing. Mama Hen, watching her little ones, felt a surge of pride. They were healing, learning to embrace life even in the face of loss. Their laughter and joy, although bittersweet, reminded her that love could endure even the deepest sorrow. As the last rays of sunlight faded, the ducklings huddled together for comfort, their wings intertwined.

They felt a sense of warmth and security in each other's presence. They knew they weren't alone, not anymore. They had each other, and they had the memories of Papa Drake, a love that would forever bind them together. The new ducklings, with their bright yellow feathers and curious eyes, approached the little group timidly. At first, the ducklings were hesitant. They still felt a deep pang of sadness in their hearts, a hollowness left by Papa Drake's absence. But Mama Hen, sensing their apprehension, gave them a gentle nudge. "Remember what Papa Drake would say?"she asked, her voice soft but firm. "He would always tell us that making new friends is a gift." The ducklings, their hearts filled with the memory of Papa Drake's kind smile and warm voice, nodded slowly. They knew he was right. Papa Drake had always loved meeting new ducks and sharing his playful energy with them. The new ducklings, sensing the hesitation, chirped excitedly, eager to play. One duckling, a bright-eyed little fellow with a fluffy white tail, waddled over to the group and chirped, "Hello! My name is Pip! What are your names?" The ducklings, feeling the warmth of acceptance, hesitantly introduced themselves. They shared their names – Sunny, Willow, and River – and spoke about their favorite games with Papa Drake, each remembering their own special moments with their father. Sunny, the most adventurous of the ducklings, remembered the time Papa Drake had taught him how to dive for the juiciest worms at the bottom of the pond. "He would always say, "Just like a little torpedo!"" Sunny exclaimed, his eyes twinkling with memories.

Willow, the quietest of the ducklings, remembered the times she would sit with Papa Drake at the edge of the pond, watching the sun dip below the horizon, painting the sky in a kaleidoscope of colors.

"He would tell me stories about the stars," she murmured, her voice filled with a bittersweet nostalgia. River, the youngest of the ducklings, remembered the playful chases with Papa Drake. "He would let me ride on his back,"River chirped, his eyes filled with a mischievous glint, remembering the fun they had splashing in the water together. The new ducklings, enthralled by the stories, listened intently, their hearts filled with empathy. They had also lost a parent, but their memories were different. They shared their stories of their own father, a wise old duck who had taught them to build the sturdiest nests and find the tastiest berries in the forest. As they shared their stories, the ducklings felt a connection, a bond forged in the shared experience of loss. Their grief, once a heavy burden, became a shared tapestry woven with threads of love and remembrance. The sun began to set, casting long shadows over the pond. The ducklings, their hearts warmed by the warmth of companionship, waddled towards their nest, their steps lighter, their laughter more spontaneous. Mama Hen, watching them from the edge of the pond, felt a surge of pride and relief.

She knew Papa Drake would be happy to see them making new friends, learning to embrace life again. The memories of Papa Drake, once a source of sorrow, had become a comforting bridge between them, connecting them to their past and guiding them towards a future filled with hope. The next day, the ducklings gathered at the pond, eager to play with their new friends. They remembered the special spot they had created for Papa Drake, a place where they could share their stories and keep his memory alive. They decided to include their new friends in their ritual, sharing their memories of Papa Drake and creating a space where they could all come together to celebrate the love and friendship that had been woven into their lives. As the days turned into weeks, the ducklings found themselves laughing more often, their hearts lighter with the shared joy of friendship. They learned that even in the face of loss, life continued, filled with new experiences, new friendships, and new adventures. One evening, as the sun painted the sky in hues of orange and purple, the ducklings gathered around their nest. They shared their stories of the day, their laughter echoing across the pond. Mama Hen, watching them, felt a wave of gratitude wash over her. She realized that Papa Drake, though physically gone, was still present in their hearts, in the way they loved each other, in the way they embraced life's challenges with courage and resilience. She knew that Papa Drake's legacy of love and laughter would continue to shine through them, guiding them towards a brighter future

The ducklings huddled closer to Mama Hen, their small bodies trembling with a mixture of fear and sadness. They had never seen their Mama cry before, her usually bright eyes now filled with tears. "Mama, why is Papa Drake gone?"Pip, the smallest duckling, asked, his voice quivering. Mama Hen took a deep breath, her voice soft and gentle. "Papa Drake is gone, my little one. But his love for us will always be here, just like the memories we made together." She ruffled Pip's soft feathers, trying to soothe his fear. "Remember how much fun we had swimming in the pond with him? He loved to chase us and make us laugh," she said, her voice cracking slightly. "I remember,"chirped Puddles, the most adventurous of the ducklings. "He would always dive and splash water on us!" "And he taught us how to catch fish!"added Quackers, the oldest and wisest duckling. The ducklings shared their memories of Papa Drake, each one a precious treasure in their hearts. They recalled his warm, comforting presence, his playful antics, and the way he always made them feel safe and loved. "Papa Drake would want us to be happy,"Mama Hen said, her eyes shining with a new light. "He would want us to make new friends and laugh together, just like we used to." The ducklings looked at each other, their sadness slowly giving way to hope. Maybe making new friends could help fill the emptiness in their hearts.

Maybe, just maybe, they could find laughter and joy again, even without Papa Drake. "I think Papa Drake would like the new ducklings," said Pip, pointing to a group of ducklings on the other side of the pond. They were playing a game of tag, their cheerful calls echoing across the water. Mama Hen smiled. "I think you're right, Pip. They seem like friendly ducklings. Maybe we could go say hello."The ducklings hesitated, their small hearts still heavy with grief. But the thought of making new friends and sharing laughter together gave them a glimmer of hope. They waddled towards the other ducklings, their small bodies filled with a mix of nervousness and anticipation. As they approached, the new ducklings stopped playing and stared at the little family. The ducklings, filled with a sudden shyness, stopped in their tracks, unsure of how to greet the new ducklings. A young duckling, with a bright yellow beak, stepped forward. "Hi,"he said, his voice cheerful. "My name is Sunny. What are your names?" "I'm Pip,"said the smallest duckling, his fear fading a bit. "I'm Puddles," chirped the adventurous one. "And I'm Quackers,"said the oldest, his voice a bit more confident now. "It's nice to meet you,"said Sunny. "We're new to the pond, and we don't know many ducks yet. "We're new here too," said Puddles. "We just lost our dad, and we've been feeling kind of sad."Sunny's smile faltered slightly. "Oh, I'm sorry," he said, "Losing someone is really hard." He paused for a moment, then added, "My grandpa died last year, and I miss him a lot." The ducklings were surprised. Sunny seemed to understand how they felt. Maybe, just maybe, these new ducklings could be their friends. "Do you want to play with us?"asked Pip, his voice hopeful. "We used to play tag with our dad, and it was so much fun." "Sure!"exclaimed Sunny. "We can play tag too! It's one of my favorite games." The ducklings and Sunny joined hands, their sadness temporarily forgotten as they ran and giggled, their playful calls echoing across the pond. They shared stories about their families, their favorite games, and their dreams for the future.

The ducklings learned that Sunny and his friends were a friendly and kind bunch. They were eager to make new friends, and they shared their own stories of loss and resilience. The ducklings found comfort in knowing that they weren't alone in their grief. As the sun began to set, casting long shadows across the pond, the ducklings gathered together, their laughter fading into a peaceful silence. They felt a renewed sense of hope and belonging. "It's good to have new friends,"Pip said, his voice soft. "Even though we miss Papa Drake, we can still be happy." "And Papa Drake would want us to be happy,"added Puddles. Quackers nodded, his eyes filled with a new light. "Papa Drake's love will always be with us, and we can carry it in our hearts, no matter what."The ducklings looked at each other, their hearts filled with a mix of sadness and hope. They knew that losing Papa Drake had left a gaping hole in their lives, but they also knew that love and memories could last even after someone is gone. They gathered around Mama Hen, her warm feathers a source of comfort, and snuggled close to her. They felt safe and loved, even though Papa Drake was no longer physically present. As they drifted off to sleep, the ducklings dreamt of Papa Drake, his playful smile, and the warmth of his love. They dreamt of new adventures and the joy of friendship. They dreamt of a future filled with hope and laughter.

The ducklings knew that life would never be the same without Papa Drake, but they also knew that love and memories could last forever. They had each other, they had new friends, and they had the strength to carry Papa Drake's love in their hearts, even in the face of loss The ducklings, at first, were hesitant. They weren't sure they were ready to make new friends. The loss of Papa Drake had left a big hole in their hearts, and they feared that anyone new couldn't possibly fill it. But Mama Hen, with her gentle patience, encouraged them. She reminded them that Papa Drake had always said that making new friends was one of life's greatest joys. One afternoon, a group of ducklings, their feathers a vibrant shade of blue and green, waddled up to the family's nest. Their eyes sparkled with curiosity, and their voices were filled with laughter. At first, the little ducklings stayed huddled together, unsure of how to respond. But Mama Hen, with her calming presence, introduced them to the new arrivals. She told them stories of Papa Drake, describing his love for his family and how he would have been delighted to meet these new friends. The new ducklings, with their infectious energy, began to play games with the others. They chased each other across the pond, their laughter echoing through the reeds. They taught the little ducklings new games and songs, filling their days with a new kind of joy.

As the days turned into weeks, the ducklings started to feel a change within them. They still missed Papa Drake, the ache in their hearts wasn't gone, but it was beginning to soften. They began to understand that it was okay to laugh and play again, to embrace new experiences and make new memories. One day, while the ducklings were playing tag with their new friends, they stumbled upon a patch of wildflowers. The flowers were a kaleidoscope of color, and the scent of their petals filled the air. As they ran through the field, one of the little ducklings discovered a tiny, delicate feather nestled amongst the blooms. It was a beautiful feather, soft and white, and it seemed to glow in the sunlight. "Do you think it's one of Papa Drake's feathers?"asked one of the ducklings, her voice tinged with sadness. The others nodded, their eyes tracing the curve of the feather. They remembered how Papa Drake had taught them to admire the beauty of nature, to appreciate the small wonders that surrounded them. Mama Hen, seeing the sadness in their eyes, gently picked up the feather. She told them that even though Papa Drake was gone, he was always with them, in their hearts and in the beauty of the world around them. She explained that Papa Drake would want them to be happy, to embrace new experiences, and to cherish the memories they had made together. That evening, the ducklings gathered together at their special spot by the pond, the feather resting gently in their midst. They shared stories of Papa Drake, remembering his love for them and his playful nature.

They talked about the new games they had learned, the laughter they had shared with their new friends, and the beautiful feather they had found. As they sat there, the setting sun casting a golden glow over the pond, they realized something profound. Even though Papa

Drake was gone, his love for them lived on. They could feel it in the warmth of the sun, in the gentle breeze that rustled through the leaves, and in the laughter that echoed through the air. The ducklings understood that Papa Drake would want them to live their lives with joy and love, to embrace new adventures and create new memories. He would want them to find happiness, even in the face of sadness. And as they sat there, their hearts filled with love and hope, they knew that Papa Drake would always be with them, watching over them and guiding them on their journey.

4

THE WHISPERING
WIND

The sun dipped low in the sky, casting long shadows across the pond. The ducklings, usually so full of energy, sat huddled together, their little bodies trembling slightly. They missed Papa Drake. He was gone, and a heavy silence had settled over their lives. The wind, whispering through the reeds, rustled the leaves of the willow tree, making a soft, sighing sound. The ducklings, their hearts full of longing, listened intently. "Do you think that's Papa's voice?"Pip, the youngest duckling, whispered, his voice barely a breath. The others looked at each other, their eyes filled with a mixture of sadness and hope. They wanted to believe it was Papa Drake's voice, a message from beyond the pond, carrying his love and reassurance. "Maybe," chirped Penny, the middle duckling. "Maybe he's telling us not to be sad." They closed their eyes, trying to hear through the rustling leaves, through the gentle breeze that carried the scent of wildflowers. They imagined his deep, comforting voice, his playful quack, his words of encouragement. "Remember how Papa used to teach us to swim?" Quacker, the oldest duckling, said, his voice soft but steady. "He always said we were the bravest, strongest ducklings in the whole pond," Penny added, a flicker of a smile gracing her beak. "And he taught us to dive for the best fish!" Pip exclaimed, his eyes sparkling with a memory of Papa Drake's patient guidance.

The wind seemed to sigh again, carrying with it the scent of Papa Drake's favorite reeds, the ones he always nibbled on before joining them for their evening swim. The ducklings remembered his gentle touch, the warmth of his feathers as he nestled them under his wing on cold nights. They huddled closer, sharing their memories, holding onto the comforting warmth of their love for Papa Drake. It was a quiet, bittersweet moment, filled with both sadness and a deep, abiding love. The sun had set, painting the sky with streaks of orange and purple. The stars began to appear, tiny pinpricks of light against the vast darkness. The ducklings, their eyes heavy with sleep, looked up at the sky, their hearts filled with the whispers of the wind, the memories of Papa Drake's love. They knew, even in his absence, his love was still a part of them, a warm, comforting presence in their hearts. As they drifted off to sleep, nestled together under Mama Hen's wing, the ducklings felt a sense of peace. They knew that even though they missed Papa Drake terribly, they were surrounded by love, and they were strong enough to face anything that came their way. They knew, deep in their hearts, that Papa Drake would always be with them, in the whispering wind, in the rustling leaves, in their memories, in their love. The ducklings huddled together by the pond, their little bodies shivering in the cool breeze.

They missed Papa Drake so much. It felt like he was always there, just out of sight, yet they couldn't see him. His absence was like a hole in their hearts, leaving behind an ache they couldn't explain. Suddenly, a whisper of wind danced through the reeds, rustling the leaves around them. The ducklings tilted their heads, listening closely. It sounded like a voice, a familiar, comforting voice. "Don't be sad, my little ducklings," the voice seemed to say."I'm always with you, even if you can't see me. Remember all the fun we had together? Remember the time we played hide-and-seek in the reeds?" The ducklings remembered. They remembered how Papa Drake would dive under the water, his bright yellow bill disappearing beneath the surface, before popping up in the most unexpected places. They'd giggle and splash as they tried to find him, their hearts full of joy. "I love you all so much,"the voice continued. "Be brave, my ducklings. Be strong. You can do anything you set your minds to." The ducklings felt a warmth spread through their bodies, a sense of peace and security. It was like Papa Drake was wrapping them in his love, a love that transcended distance and time. "Remember how I taught you to fly?" the voice whispered. "Remember how I encouraged you to be brave and face your fears? You are all amazing little ducks, capable of so much. Don't ever forget that." The ducklings felt a surge of courage. They remembered how Papa Drake had taught them to spread their wings and soar through the air, even though they were afraid at first. They remembered how he'd been there, cheering them on, telling them they could do it. "You are all so special," the voice whispered, "and I am so proud of each and every one of you." The ducklings felt a rush of emotion, tears welling up in their eyes. They missed Papa Drake terribly, but they also felt his love surrounding them, like a warm blanket on a cold day. It was a love that would never fade, a love that would always be with them.

"I'll always be watching over you," the voice whispered gently. "And I'll always be with you, in your hearts."The ducklings knew it was true. Even though they couldn't see Papa Drake, they could feel his love in their hearts. They knew he was with them, always. And that gave them the strength to face whatever came their way. They looked at each other, their eyes shining with a new sense of hope. They knew they could do anything they set their minds to, because Papa Drake's love was always with them, guiding them and encouraging them. They were brave, strong, and capable, just like Papa Drake had always told them. The ducklings, emboldened by Papa Drake's love, decided to honor his memory. They would live their lives to the fullest, just like he would have wanted. They would embrace their fears and learn to fly, knowing that even though he was gone, he was always with them in spirit. As the sun began to set, casting long shadows across the pond, the ducklings gathered around Papa Drake's special spot by the water.

It was a small clearing under a willow tree, a place where they could come to remember him. They took turns sharing their favorite memories of Papa Drake, their voices filled with laughter and tears. They remembered his funny antics, his gentle words, and the love he had showered upon them. They felt a sense of peace and comfort knowing that even though Papa Drake was gone, his love lived on in their hearts. As the stars twinkled in the night sky, the ducklings snuggled together for warmth, their little bodies close. They felt a sense of gratitude for the time they had with Papa Drake, and they knew that his love would forever be a part of them The ducklings sat by the pond, the water shimmering like a thousand tiny jewels under the afternoon sun. A gentle breeze rustled through the reeds, whispering secrets only the wind could hear. But the ducklings weren't listening to the wind's tales; they were listening to the whispers of their hearts, the echoes of a love that still resonated deep within them. They missed Papa Drake more than words could say. They missed his playful dives and his booming quack that always filled the air with laughter. They missed the warmth of his feathers, the gentle nudge of his beak, and the feeling of being safe under his watchful gaze. A tear slipped down Pip's cheek, a silent testament to the ache that lived in his little heart. He looked at his siblings, their faces reflecting his own sorrow, their eyes mirroring the sadness that had settled over their family. It felt like a heavy cloak, smothering their joy and dimming the light in their hearts.

Suddenly, a memory flickered in Pip's mind, like a spark igniting a forgotten flame. He remembered a day, not too long ago, when Papa Drake had taken them on a daring adventure. The water was choppy, the wind was strong, and the waves threatened to toss them about like small boats. But Papa Drake had stayed calm, his voice a steady beacon in the storm. "Fear is a trickster, my little ones," Papa Drake had said, his eyes twinkling with wisdom. "It whispers doubts and doubts, making you think you are weak. But you are strong, you are brave, and you are loved." His words echoed in Pip's mind, reminding him of the courage Papa Drake had instilled in them. Papa Drake had always taught them to face their fears, to be bold and confident, to embrace the challenges of life with a smile and a determined heart. "We can do this, Pip," said Penny, her voice filled with newfound strength. "Papa Drake taught us to be brave. We can be brave too."The others chimed in, their voices echoing Penny's sentiment.

The memory of Papa Drake's words, his love, and his faith in them, ignited a spark of hope in their hearts. They were not alone; Papa Drake's love was with them, even in his absence. His spirit, his wisdom, his love - these were the things that would guide them through their sadness. As the sun dipped below the horizon, painting the sky in hues of orange and purple, the ducklings felt a sense of comfort wash over them. The whispering wind seemed to carry a message of love, a gentle reminder that even in the face of loss, life went on. They were still a family, bound together by the unbreakable threads of love and memory."Let's go to Papa Drake's place,"said Peter, his voice full of determination."Let's tell him about our day, share our memories, and sing him our favorite song." They waddled towards the special spot by the pond where they had gathered to remember Papa Drake, the place where they had left a collection of smooth pebbles, each one representing a cherished memory of their father. They sat in a circle, the setting sun casting long shadows around them. They shared stories, laughter, and tears, their voices weaving a tapestry of love and remembrance. They sang their favorite songs, their voices echoing through the tranquil evening air. The wind seemed to listen, carrying their voices on its gentle wings, whispering their love and gratitude to the heavens. And in the stillness of the twilight, they felt a profound sense of peace, knowing that Papa Drake's love was a constant, a guiding light that would always illuminate their path. Even though he was gone, he was always with them, a comforting presence in their hearts, a love that transcended the boundaries of time and space. His spirit lived on in their courage, their strength, and their unyielding love for each other.

The ducklings gathered at the pond, their little heads bobbing in unison as they felt the weight of their sadness. The sun, which had been a joyful presence before Papa Drake's absence, seemed to dim in sympathy. It was a quiet day, with only the gentle whisper of the wind rustling through the reeds, carrying with it a faint echo of their father's laughter. "Do you remember how Papa Drake used to make us laugh?"Pip, the smallest duckling, said, his voice tinged with sadness. "He would dip his beak into the water and splash us, making us all shiver and squawk.""And he always knew how to make the best mud pies,"said Penny, the second smallest, her eyes welling up with tears. "He would help us mold them into funny shapes and decorate them with sticks and pebbles." "He taught us how to swim in the deep end,"added Percy, the eldest, his voice a little stronger, but still tinged with grief. "He said we just had to believe in ourselves and trust the water." The memories flowed freely now, each one a precious jewel, reminding them of the love and joy Papa Drake had brought into their lives. They recalled his gentle quacks, his patient guidance, his playful spirit that had filled their days with sunshine. "Remember how he would sing us lullabies before bedtime?" asked Polly, her voice soft and sweet. "His voice was like a warm breeze, and it would lull us to sleep, making us feel safe and loved." "He loved us all so much," said Mama Hen, her voice thick with emotion. "And he would want us to be happy, even without him." The ducklings looked at their mother, their hearts heavy with the weight of their grief, but they knew she was right. Papa Drake would want them to be happy. He would want them to keep his memory alive, to celebrate the joy he had brought into their lives.

An idea sparked in Penny's eyes, a glimmer of hope piercing through their sadness. "We could have a party for Papa Drake!"she exclaimed. "We could tell stories about him, sing his favorite songs, and remember all the good times we had together."The other ducklings, their eyes brightening with understanding, quickly embraced the idea. They knew that while Papa Drake was gone, his love and memory lived on in their hearts. And celebrating his life was a way to honor him, to keep his spirit alive. The next day, the ducklings gathered at their special spot by the pond. It was a small clearing, surrounded by reeds and willows, where they had placed a smooth, flat stone as a marker for Papa Drake. "He would have loved this place,"said Pip, looking around at the quiet, serene spot. "He would have loved the peace and the beauty of it,"; added Percy, his voice calmer now, his sadness gradually replaced by a sense of acceptance. They sat in a circle around the stone, each taking turns sharing stories of Papa Drake. They spoke of his kindness, his patience, his unwavering love for them. They laughed as they recalled his funny antics and his playful spirit. "He was the best dad a duckling could ask for,"said Polly, her voice full of admiration. "And he was the best husband a duck could ask for," Mama Hen added softly, a tear rolling down her cheek. As they shared their memories, the sadness gradually faded, replaced by a sense of warmth and gratitude. They realized that even though Papa Drake was gone, his love was still present in their hearts, a constant reminder of the joy he had brought into their lives.

They then started singing Papa Drake's favorite song, a simple melody that he had taught them, a song that always made them feel happy and loved. They sang with their hearts, their voices blending together in a sweet harmony, a tribute to their beloved father. As the sun began to set, casting long shadows across the pond, the ducklings knew that they had done something special. They had celebrated Papa Drake's life, they had remembered him with love, and they had found a way to move forward, carrying his love in their hearts. And as the stars twinkled above, the ducklings, nestled together for the night, knew that Papa Drake would always be with them, in the whispering wind, in the rustling leaves, in the warm sunlight, and most importantly, in the love they shared. The ducklings huddled together, their small bodies trembling slightly in the cool evening breeze. They looked out at the pond, its surface shimmering under the fading sunlight. The water, usually so full of life and laughter, seemed strangely quiet tonight. A gentle wind rustled the reeds at the edge of the pond, sending whispers through the air. The ducklings listened intently, their hearts pounding with a mixture of sadness and hope. They remembered how Papa Drake, their beloved father, used to tell them stories about the wind. He would say that the wind carried messages from faraway lands, and that it whispered secrets to those who listened carefully. "Do you think Papa Drake is whispering to us now?" asked Pip, the smallest of the ducklings. His voice was barely a whisper, filled with longing and a hint of fear. "I think he is," replied Poppy, her older sister. "He's telling us he's okay, and that he loves us." The ducklings closed their eyes, trying to listen to the whispers of the wind. They imagined Papa Drake's warm voice, filled with love and reassurance. They remembered his gentle quacks, his playful dives, and the way he always knew just how to make them laugh.

"He taught us to be brave,"said Penny, the middle duckling. "He said that even when things are tough, we should never give up hope." The ducklings remembered how Papa Drake had encouraged them to try new things, to be brave, and to never lose sight of their dreams. They recalled his wise words, his loving eyes, and the way he always made them feel safe and loved. Suddenly, a gust of wind swept across the pond, carrying the scent of wildflowers and the soft chirping of crickets. It felt like a gentle hug, a warm embrace from Papa Drake. "He's saying goodbye," said Pip, his voice trembling with emotion. "No, Pip,"said Mama Hen, her voice soft and soothing. "He's saying hello. He's saying he's with us, always. He's in our hearts." The ducklings looked up at Mama Hen, their eyes filled with confusion and a glimmer of understanding. They realized that Papa Drake was gone, but his love and memories remained. He was in their hearts, in every playful splash, every gentle whisper of the wind, and every warm ray of sunshine. "He's with us in the whispers of the wind," said Poppy. "And in the laughter of the pond," added Penny. The ducklings looked at each other, their eyes filled with a newfound sense of peace. They understood that even though Papa Drake was physically gone, his love and spirit lived on in their hearts. They could still feel his presence, his warmth, and his unwavering love.

They decided to celebrate Papa Drake's life. They would gather by the pond, under the shimmering moonlight, and share their stories and memories. They would sing his favorite songs, tell his favorite jokes, and remember the joy he brought into their lives. The ducklings felt a sense of unity and love as they huddled closer together, their tiny hearts filled with the memories of their beloved father. They knew that even though Papa Drake was gone, he would always be with them, in the whispers of the wind, in their laughter, and in the warmth of their hearts. His love would forever be a beacon of light, guiding them through the darkness and reminding them that even in the face of loss, hope and love could always prevail.

5

THE SUN SHINES
AGAIN

The season changed, and with it, the pond transformed. The water, once a mirror reflecting the somber sky, now shimmered with the vibrant hues of spring. Lush green reeds swayed gently in the breeze, and the air buzzed with the joyful symphony of birdsong. Tiny fish darted through the clear water, chasing each other in a game of hide- and-seek. The pond, once a silent testament to their loss, was now brimming with new life, a vibrant reminder of the world's unending cycle of renewal. The ducklings, though still carrying the weight of their grief, were adapting to their new reality. They no longer huddled together in the nest, their small bodies trembling with fear and sadness. They had learned to navigate the world without their beloved Papa Drake, their wings finding a new strength in their shared sorrow. One sunny morning, the ducklings gathered at the edge of the pond, their eyes wide with wonder. The water was still, reflecting the golden glow of the rising sun.

A gentle breeze rustled the leaves, whispering secrets only they could hear. "Do you remember when Papa Drake taught us to swim?" asked Pip, the smallest duckling, his voice a soft whisper. The other ducklings, nestled close together, nodded their tiny heads. Memories flickered in their eyes – Papa Drake's encouraging voice, the joyous splash of water, and the warmth of his presence. "I miss his big, strong wings," said Dot, her eyes welling up with tears. "I miss his funny quack," added Quack, a hint of sadness in his voice. "Me too," the other ducklings murmured, their hearts echoing the same ache of loss. Mama Hen, watching her ducklings from a distance, her heart ached with a love that was both bittersweet and enduring. She knew the pain they felt, the emptiness that lingered in their hearts. But she also saw the resilience in their spirits, the glimmer of hope that shone in their eyes. "Papa Drake was a special duck,"she said softly, her voice a soothing balm to their wounded hearts. "He loved you all very much, and he would want you to be happy." She gathered her ducklings close, sharing their memories of Papa Drake. They remembered the countless games they played, the hilarious antics that made them laugh until their sides ached, and the warmth of his love that enveloped them like a comforting blanket. Each memory, though tinged with sadness, brought a smile to their faces, a flicker of joy amidst the pain.

One by one, the ducklings began to venture out, their small bodies testing the water with tentative dips. They remembered Papa Drake's guidance, his gentle encouragement, and the thrill of their first successful attempts at swimming. The water, once a source of fear, now felt invigorating, a reminder of their growing strength and resilience. They learned to fly, their small wings beating against the wind, their eyes fixed on the boundless sky. They soared high above the pond, feeling a sense of liberation they had never known before. The world stretched before them, filled with endless possibilities. Papa Drake's memory was always present, a constant in their lives. They visited his special spot by the pond regularly, sharing their stories, their hopes, and their dreams. The space, once filled with sorrow, had become a place of peace and reflection, a sacred sanctuary where they could feel close to their beloved Papa Drake.. One day, as the sun dipped below the horizon, painting the sky in hues of orange and gold, Mama Hen gathered her ducklings around her. She looked into their eyes, seeing the reflection of Papa Drake's love and the enduring strength of their spirit. "Life is full of surprises," she said softly. "Sometimes, it brings us great joy, and sometimes, it brings us sorrow. But even when we are sad, we can still find happiness. We can still learn, we can still grow, and we can still love.";Her ducklings listened, their hearts filled with a mixture of sadness and hope. They knew they would always miss Papa Drake, his presence a permanent void in their lives. But they also knew that their love for him would never fade.

"Remember," Mama Hen continued, "Papa Drake's love is with us always, even though he is not here. It's in the gentle breeze, the warmth of the sun, and the love we share with each other. We will carry him in our hearts, and his memory will guide us." As the stars twinkled above, the ducklings huddled together, their hearts filled with a newfound peace. They had learned that even in the face of loss, life continues to flow, a river carrying them through the currents of grief and hope. They had learned that love, like the enduring cycle of nature, can bloom even in the darkest of times. They had learned that even though Papa Drake was gone, his love remained a beacon of light in the ever-changing landscape of their lives. The days that followed were filled with new experiences, each one a little bit different than before. Mama Hen, wise and strong as always, encouraged the ducklings to explore the pond. "Papa Drake would want you to be brave,"she said, her voice soft and gentle. "He always loved adventure."The ducklings, remembering their father's playful spirit, took her words to heart. They ventured out to the far edge of the pond, where the water lilies grew thick and tall, their leaves like green islands on the water's surface. They dipped their beaks into the cool water, catching tiny insects and learning the secrets of the pond's depths. Then came the day they learned to fly. Mama Hen, with her wings spread wide, soared above the pond, her feathers catching the sunlight. She called out to her ducklings, encouraging them to follow. One by one, they took a leap of faith, flapping their wings with all their might.

At first, they wobbled and stumbled, their little bodies struggling to stay aloft. But Mama Hen was there, guiding them gently, her voice a steady reassurance in the air. Gradually, they gained confidence. They soared above the pond, their wings beating strong and steady. The wind ruffled their feathers, carrying the scent of wildflowers and fresh earth. From their new vantage point, they saw the world in a different way. The pond was no longer just a familiar haven; it was a vast, exciting expanse, full of possibilities. They soared above the willow trees, their branches swaying gently in the breeze. They flew over the reeds, their soft whispers carrying Papa Drake's memory. The ducklings realized that life, even without their father, was full of joy and wonder. They discovered new places, new smells, new sights, and new friendships. Each day brought a new adventure, a new challenge, a new learning experience. They learned to navigate the currents of the pond, to dodge the playful splashes of other ducks, and to find their way back to the nest safely. They made new friends, too. A family of geese with goslings, their honking calls echoing through the air. A group of playful muskrats, their whiskers twitching as they scurried along the banks of the pond. These new companions brought laughter and companionship into their lives, filling the silence left by their father's absence. But even as they embraced the new, the ducklings never forgot Papa Drake. They visited his special spot by the pond often, where the sunlight filtered through the leaves of a towering oak tree. They sat in the cool shade, sharing their stories and memories of their father. They held onto his feather, smooth and soft against their skin, a tangible reminder of his love and presence in their lives. "He loved to watch us play," one duckling said, his voice filled with nostalgia.

"Remember how he would splash us with his beak, making us squeal with laughter?" "And how he would tell us stories about the stars, pointing them out in the night sky," another duckling chimed in. "He said that each star was a little piece of his love, watching over us." They shared stories of their father's kindness, his strength, his love for his family. They remembered how he would protect them from harm, how he would teach them how to swim, how he would sing them songs to lull them to sleep. The ducklings realized that even though their father was gone, his love remained. It lived in their hearts, in their memories, in their shared stories. It was a comforting presence, guiding them through the ups and downs of life, reminding them that they were loved, cherished, and never truly alone. As the seasons changed, the ducklings continued to grow and learn. They embraced the future, their hearts filled with a mixture of sadness and joy. They learned that life is a journey, full of surprises and challenges, and that love, like a bright and beautiful light, can guide us through even the darkest of times. They knew that they would always miss their father, but they also knew that he would always be with them. In the whispering wind, in the rustling leaves, in the warmth of the sun, they could feel his love, his presence, his spirit, guiding them on their way. The ducklings, remembering Papa Drake's gentle nature and the joy he brought them, started visiting his special spot by the pond more often. It wasn't a sad place, not anymore. It was a place where they felt close to him, where the gentle breeze whispered stories of his love and the sunbeams danced in patterns that reminded them of his playful spirit. They would gather around the large, flat rock where Papa Drake used to sit and watch them play.

Each duckling would share a memory, a funny anecdote, a moment of pure joy they had experienced with him. They spoke of the time Papa Drake had taught them how to swim, patiently guiding them with his strong webbed feet. They remembered how he would waddle around the pond, quacking with delight as he chased after the shiny pebbles, his feathery tail bouncing with each step. Sometimes, Mama Hen would join them, her eyes filled with a mixture of sadness and warmth. She would share stories of Papa Drake's bravery, his kindness, and his unwavering love for his family. She told them how he had always put their needs before his own, how he would tirelessly gather the tastiest reeds for them and how he would stay up all night, keeping them warm with his feathery embrace. These moments by the pond, filled with laughter and tearful reminiscing, became a special ritual for the ducklings. They understood that remembering Papa Drake wasn't about dwelling on their loss, but about celebrating his life, cherishing the love he gave them, and carrying his spirit within their hearts. It was during one of these quiet evenings, as the sun dipped below the horizon, casting long shadows over the pond, that the ducklings noticed something peculiar. A small, iridescent feather, a glimmering blue and green, drifted down from the sky, landing gently on the rock where they sat. "It's like a little piece of Papa Drake," whispered one duckling, its voice trembling with a mixture of awe and sadness. The other ducklings nodded in agreement, their eyes wide with wonder. The feather, shimmering in the fading light, seemed to radiate a gentle warmth, as if carrying a message of love and hope. They carefully picked up the feather, holding it close to their chests, their hearts overflowing with a bittersweet joy.

They knew that Papa Drake would always be with them, in their hearts, in their memories, and now, even in this delicate, shimmering reminder of his presence. As they held onto the feather, feeling the weight of their grief and the warmth of their love, the ducklings realized something profound. Their journey of healing wasn't about forgetting Papa Drake, but about finding a way to live with the memory of his love, even though he wasn't physically present. They understood that life, like the pond they called home, was a constant cycle of change and renewal. Papa Drake's absence was a painful part of that cycle, but their love for him, like the unwavering flow of the pond, would never cease. The ducklings, emboldened by their shared memories and strengthened by their newfound understanding, decided to create a little ceremony to honor Papa Drake. They collected a handful of bright, colorful pebbles and arranged them around the feather on the rock, forming a heart. It was their way of saying thank you to Papa Drake, for the love he had given them, for the lessons he had taught them, and for the memories he had left behind. The sun, bidding farewell for the night, cast a golden glow over the pond, illuminating the heart of pebbles and the feather that rested at its center.

The ducklings, watching the sun sink below the horizon, felt a sense of peace settling over them.

They knew that their lives would never be the same without Papa Drake, but they also knew that they would carry his love and his spirit with them, always, and that love, like the sun, would always find a way to shine through, even on the cloudiest of days. As the stars began to appear in the darkening sky, the ducklings waddled back to their nest, their hearts full of memories and their eyes filled with a quiet hope. They knew that their journey of healing was just beginning, but they also knew that they had each other, their love for Papa Drake, and the unwavering belief that even in the face of loss, love and hope would always find a way to prevail. The sun peeked through the clouds, casting warm rays on the pond. It was a new season, the air buzzing with the sounds of spring. The ducklings, though still missing Papa Drake dearly, felt a shift within them. They were beginning to understand that life continued even after loss. While the ache in their hearts remained, a new spark of hope ignited within them. The pond was a vibrant tapestry of color, the water shimmering with life. New ducklings paddled alongside them, their chirps echoing with youthful energy. The ducklings, once shy and withdrawn, now found themselves drawn to the playful energy of their new companions. They giggled as they chased each other through the reeds, their laughter echoing across the pond. One day, as they were exploring a secluded corner of the pond, they stumbled upon a patch of wild flowers. The blossoms were a riot of color – vibrant reds, sunny yellows, and delicate blues.

The ducklings had never seen anything so beautiful. "Wow!" exclaimed one duckling, his eyes wide with wonder. "It's like Papa Drake is here, making the world more beautiful.""He is," whispered another duckling. "He's in our hearts, and he makes everything beautiful." Mama Hen, watching her ducklings from a distance, smiled warmly. She saw the joy returning to their eyes, the laughter replacing the sadness. They were learning to thrive, to find happiness in new experiences, even though they still missed Papa Drake dearly. They visited Papa Drake's special spot by the pond regularly, a small clearing by the willow tree where they had shared stories and laughter. They placed the feather there, a tangible reminder of their beloved Papa Drake. As they sat there, they shared their memories, whispering stories of Papa Drake's playful antics and his gentle love. The place, once filled with grief, now became a sanctuary of peace and reflection. The ducklings learned that remembering Papa Drake didn't mean dwelling on their sadness. It meant cherishing the memories, celebrating his life, and carrying his love in their hearts. They learned that their love for him was as enduring as the pond itself, a constant presence that guided them through the ups and downs of life. One evening, as the sun painted the sky in hues of orange and purple, the ducklings sat by the pond, watching the clouds drift by. They felt a sense of peace settling over them. "Do you think Papa Drake is happy?" asked one duckling, his voice soft. "He is,"said another duckling. "He's happy because we're happy."And they were. They were still sad, but they were also happy. They were living their lives, embracing the future with open hearts, carrying Papa Drake's love and memories with them wherever they went. They had learned that even though loss is painful, it is possible to live a happy and fulfilling life. They were a testament to the enduring power of love and hope, a family bound by the love they shared for their Papa Drake, and the beautiful memories they had made together. The ducklings, with their fluffy feathers ruffled by the gentle breeze, felt a sense of peace settle over them. They had learned that life was full of surprises, some joyful and some bittersweet. They had learned that even though Papa Drake was gone, his love was always with them. It was a feeling they carried in their hearts, like a warm sunbeam on a cold day. They knew they would never forget Papa Drake, his playful dives in the pond, his soft quacks that echoed through the reeds, and the warmth of his feathers when they huddled close together in their nest. Papa Drake's spirit lived on in their memories, and in the love they shared. The ducklings found joy in the simple things now.

A playful splash in the pond, a race across the grassy meadow, the taste of juicy berries they found under the willow trees, all brought smiles to their little faces. They were learning to thrive, just like Papa Drake would have wanted them to. Mama Hen continued to be their rock, her wise eyes watching over them, guiding them through the ups and downs of their lives. She was their anchor, their source of comfort, and their unwavering love. One afternoon, the ducklings gathered by the pond. The sun was warm on their backs, the wind rustled through the reeds, and the water glistened like a thousand tiny diamonds. They sat in a circle, their heads tilted slightly, listening to the gentle lapping of the water against the bank. "Do you ever miss Papa Drake?" asked one of the ducklings, his voice barely a whisper. "Of course, we miss him every day," said Mama Hen, her voice soft and gentle. "But his love is always with us, in our hearts, in our memories. It's a love that never goes away, even if he's not here with us physically." The ducklings thought about this for a moment, their little heads bobbing. They understood what Mama Hen meant. Papa Drake's love was a part of them, woven into the fabric of their being. It was the warmth that kept them going, the strength that helped them face their fears, and the joy that filled their hearts. The ducklings looked at each other, their eyes sparkling with a shared understanding.

They knew that life would never be the same without Papa Drake. But they also knew that they could still live a happy and fulfilling life, carrying his love in their hearts. They would always cherish the memories they shared, and they would always remember him with love. They were a family, bound together by their shared experiences, their love for each other, and the love they had for Papa Drake. And they knew that even though life had taken him away, they would continue to love and cherish each other, just as Papa Drake had loved them. And so, the ducklings continued to swim in the pond, explore the world around them, and build new memories. They learned to fly, to play, and to find joy in the simple things. And they knew that even in their darkest moments, they would always have Papa Drake's love to guide them, to comfort them, and to remind them that they were loved. For love, like the sun that warmed their little feathers, had a way of shining even through the darkest of clouds. And as they learned to live with love, they discovered that even though loss was painful, it was also possible to find happiness, hope, and a new beginning.

6

PAPA DRAKE'S RAINBOW

The sun peeked through the clouds, painting the pond with shimmering light. The ducklings, huddled together near the water's edge, were captivated by the spectacle unfolding above them. A magnificent rainbow arced across the sky, its vibrant colors stretching from one end of the horizon to the other. It was a breathtaking sight, a kaleidoscope of beauty that left them speechless. "Oh Mama Hen," chirped one of the ducklings, her voice filled with awe. "Look! It's like magic!" The other ducklings echoed her sentiment, their little heads tilted back in wonder as they gazed at the rainbow. It seemed to shimmer and pulsate, as if it were alive, its colors dancing and blending together in a mesmerizing display. Mama Hen, her heart filled with a bittersweet mixture of sadness and hope, looked up at the rainbow and smiled. She knew how much her ducklings missed their, Papa Drake. His absence left a hollow space in their hearts, a void that seemed to echo with the memory of his warm, gentle presence. But seeing their innocent faces, alight with joy at the beauty of the rainbow, gave her a glimmer of hope.

"That's a beautiful sight, isn't it?" she said, her voice soft and tender. "A rainbow is a sign of hope, a promise of new beginnings. It tells us that even when things are dark and sad, there's always a possibility for joy and beauty to return."The ducklings, their faces lit by the colors of the rainbow, listened intently to Mama Hen's words. They were still young, their understanding of the world limited, but they instinctively sensed the truth in her words. The rainbow, with its vibrant colors and ethereal beauty, seemed to symbolize something profound, something that transcended their limited understanding.

"Does Papa Drake see the rainbow too?" asked one of the ducklings, her voice filled with longing. "Is he happy there?" Mama Hen placed a comforting wing over her duckling, her eyes filled with a mixture of sadness and love. "Papa Drake is always with us," she said, her voice soft but firm. "His love is like the rainbow, bright and beautiful, even though we can't see him anymore. And whenever you see a rainbow, my little ones, just remember that it's a sign from Papa Drake, a reminder that he's always watching over you, and his love will always be with you." The ducklings, their hearts touched by Mama Hen's words, looked up at the rainbow with renewed hope. They imagined Papa Drake looking down at them from the heavens, smiling and watching over them, his love a vibrant, radiant presence in their lives. The rainbow, a symbol of hope and beauty, became a tangible reminder of Papa Drake's love, a promise that even in the face of loss, love and hope can always prevail. As the sun began to dip below the horizon, the rainbow slowly faded, its colors dissolving into the twilight sky. But its message of hope and love lingered in the ducklings' hearts, a beacon of light in the face of their grief. They knew that even though they missed Papa Drake dearly, his love would always be with them, as bright and vibrant as the rainbow that had graced their sky.

One sunny day, as the ducklings were playing by the pond, a breathtaking sight appeared in the sky. A magnificent rainbow arced across the heavens, its vibrant colors painting the clouds with streaks of red, orange, yellow, green, blue, indigo, and violet. The ducklings gasped in awe, their eyes wide with wonder as they watched the rainbow shimmer and dance in the sunlight. "Oh, Mama Hen! Look at that beautiful rainbow!"exclaimed Pip, the youngest of the ducklings, his little head tilted back in wonder. "It' so pretty, Mama!" chirped Quack, his eyes sparkling with delight. "It's like a giant bridge to the sky!" added Waddle, her beak wide with amazement. Mama Hen smiled, her heart filled with a bittersweet warmth as she looked at her ducklings' faces, lit up with wonder and joy. She knew that the rainbow held a special meaning for them, a reminder of their beloved Papa Drake. "That is a very special rainbow, my little ones,"Mama Hen said gently, her voice soft with love and remembrance. "It's a sign of hope and new beginnings, a promise from Papa Drake that he's always watching over us, even though he's gone." The ducklings looked at Mama Hen, their faces filled with a mixture of curiosity and sadness.

They had never seen a rainbow before, and they didn't fully understand what Mama Hen meant. "How can Papa Drake be watching over us if he's not here?"asked Pip, his little voice trembling slightly. Mama Hen knelt down and gently tucked Pip's head under her wing. "Love never ends, my little one,"she explained softly. "Even though Papa Drake is gone, his love for you is still here, in your hearts and in our memories. Whenever you see a rainbow, remember that it's Papa Drake's way of letting you know that he's always with you in spirit, that his love is always surrounding you."The ducklings listened intently, their eyes fixed on Mama Hen's face. They could sense the deep love and sadness in her voice, and they knew that what she said was true. Even though Papa Drake was gone, his love and presence lingered in their hearts. "So, whenever we see a rainbow, it means Papa Drake is happy?"asked Quack, a glimmer of hope lighting up his eyes. "Yes, my little one,"Mama Hen replied, her voice filled with warmth. "It means he's watching over us, sending us his love and blessings." The ducklings nodded, their faces filled with a newfound understanding. They looked back at the rainbow, now feeling a sense of comfort and peace instead of sadness. They realized that even though they missed Papa Drake dearly, his love was still very much alive in their hearts, and he was always with them in spirit. "Papa Drake loved rainbows, didn't he?" asked Waddle, her eyes twinkling with a sudden memory. "Yes, he did," Mama Hen replied with a tender smile. "He used to say that rainbows were like bridges between the earth and the sky, a symbol of hope and connection. He would often chase the rainbows, saying that they led to a magical land filled with joy and wonder."

The ducklings giggled at the memory of Papa Drake chasing rainbows, picturing his playful antics and infectious laughter. They remembered how he would tell them stories about the magical land he would find at the end of the rainbow, a place filled with sparkling rivers, singing flowers, and fluffy clouds. "Maybe he's there now, at the end of the rainbow, watching over us,"suggested Pip, a soft smile spreading across his face. "Maybe he is," agreed Mama Hen, her eyes glistening with tears of love and remembrance. "And maybe one day, we'll all meet him again at the end of the rainbow, in that magical land he told us about." The ducklings gazed at the rainbow, their hearts filled with a mixture of love, hope, and a touch of sadness. They knew that they would always miss Papa Drake dearly, but they also knew that his love was always with them, and that one day, they would meet him again, at the end of a beautiful, shimmering rainbow. As the sun began to set, casting a warm glow on the pond, the rainbow slowly faded from view. But its vibrant colors remained imprinted on the ducklings' hearts, a reminder of Papa Drake's love and the enduring power of hope. They knew that even in the face of loss, love and hope could always prevail. The ducklings gathered around Mama Hen, their little heads tilted up, their eyes filled with a mixture of sadness and curiosity. They had heard Mama Hen speak about rainbows before, but this time, it felt different. It was as if the rainbow held a special meaning, a secret message whispered from Papa Drake himself. Mama Hen smiled gently, her eyes sparkling with a hint of tears. "Rainbows are a sign of hope, little ones," she said, her voice soft and reassuring. "They remind us that even after a storm, the sun always shines again. And when you see a rainbow, it's like Papa Drake is sending you a message. He's saying,"I'm watching over you. I'm always with you. And my love for you will never end."

The ducklings, their small hearts still aching with the loss of their father, felt a warmth spread through them as they listened to Mama Hen's words. They had never seen a rainbow so bright, so beautiful, and it seemed as if Papa Drake had painted it just for them, a reminder of his love that would always stay with them. It was as if Papa Drake had whispered to them through the wind, telling them to be strong and brave, that he was always with them, even though they couldn't see him. They felt his love surrounding them, a comforting embrace that filled their little hearts with hope. The ducklings, with their hearts filled with warmth and hope, began to realize that even though they missed Papa Drake terribly, life went on. They had each other, their loving Mama Hen, and the memories of Papa Drake that filled their hearts. Papa Drake's love was a constant presence, a beacon of hope in their little world. The rainbow shimmered in the sky, a vibrant arch of colors against the backdrop of the blue sky. The ducklings watched, mesmerized by its beauty, their hearts filled with a bittersweet mix of sadness and hope. They knew they would always miss their father, but Papa Drake's rainbow showed them that his love was a part of them, a piece of his heart that they carried with them always. They realized that love was a powerful force, stronger than any storm or any sadness. They could feel Papa Drake's love in the warmth of the sun, in the gentle rustling of the leaves, and in the laughter of their new friends. His love was a reminder that even in the face of loss, hope and happiness could still bloom. They understood that Papa Drake, though gone, was still with them, in their hearts, in their memories, and in the beauty of the world around them. They would always cherish the love he gave them, and they would use that love to face the future, to find happiness and to create new memories that would be filled with love and laughter.

As the sun began to set, casting long shadows across the pond, the ducklings gathered together, their small bodies huddled close for warmth. They looked up at the fading rainbow, a reminder of Papa Drake's love and the enduring power of hope. They knew that even though they missed Papa Drake terribly, they would always find comfort in knowing that he was always with them, in their hearts, in their memories, and in the beauty of the world around them. And that, they realized, was a kind of love that would never fade. The ducklings gathered around Mama Hen, their tiny bodies huddled close. Their eyes, reflecting the colors of the rainbow, were filled with a mix of wonder and a lingering sadness. Mama Hen, her heart full of both grief and pride, watched her little ones, their small beaks chirping with questions. "Mama" one of the ducklings chirped, tilting his head towards the rainbow, "is that for Papa Drake?"Mama Hen smiled softly, her heart swelling with a mix of sadness and love. "Yes, my little one," she said, her voice soft as the gentle breeze that carried the scent of wildflowers. "Papa Drake loved rainbows. He used to tell us that whenever we saw one, it meant that someone we loved was sending us a special hug from above." The ducklings, their tiny hearts still aching with the loss of their father, felt a glimmer of comfort in this new explanation. The rainbow, once a fleeting beauty in the sky, now carried a special meaning, a reminder of Papa Drake's love that transcended even death. "But Mama,"another duckling piped up, "Papa Drake is gone. How can he send us a hug?"Mama Hen's eyes welled up, but she quickly blinked away the tears, determined to keep her voice steady. "Love, my dear, is very powerful," she explained gently, "even when someone is gone, their love doesn't disappear. It stays in our hearts, like a warm glow that never goes out. And sometimes, when we need a little reminder of their love, a rainbow appears, like a magical sign from above."As Mama Hen spoke, the ducklings gazed at the rainbow, their hearts filled with a mix of sorrow and a newfound hope. They understood that even though Papa Drake was no longer physically with them, his love for them was as bright and strong as the colors of the rainbow that arched across the sky. ";Papa Drake always said that rainbows were a promise,"Mama Hen continued, "a promise that even when things feel dark and sad, there's always a little bit of magic waiting to brighten our day. It's a reminder that love and hope can always prevail, even when things seem impossible." The ducklings listened intently, their little heads nodding in understanding. They had seen the darkness of their grief, the sadness that shadowed their hearts.

But now, as they gazed at the rainbow, they saw a different kind of light, a light that spoke of love, hope, and the enduring power of memories. "So, whenever you see a rainbow," Mama Hen concluded, "remember that it's Papa Drake's way of saying, "I love you,", and that even though he's not here with us, he's always watching over us, sending us love and happiness." The ducklings, their hearts filled with a newfound peace, embraced the beauty of the rainbow. They realized that even in the face of loss, love and hope could always prevail. Papa Drake's love, like the enduring beauty of the rainbow, would forever grace their lives, reminding them that their journey, even though it was tinged with sadness, was still filled with love, light, and the promise of brighter days to come. The ducklings, their hearts lighter than they had been in weeks, spent the rest of the afternoon playing in the pond, their laughter echoing through the air, a testament to the strength of their love and the enduring power of memories. The rainbow, a symbol of Papa Drake's love and the unwavering power of hope, faded from the sky, but its message resonated in the hearts of the ducklings, reminding them that even though their lives had changed, love and hope would always be there, guiding them through the journey ahead. The sun dipped low in the sky, painting the pond with hues of orange and purple. The ducklings, nestled comfortably amongst Mama Hen's soft feathers, watched the colors dance on the water. They were no longer the wide-eyed, clumsy little ducklings who had once followed Papa Drake everywhere. They had grown, both physically and emotionally. The fear and confusion that had once filled their hearts had softened into a quiet sadness, a gentle ache that lingered in their memories.

Today, a warm breeze carried a sweet scent of honeysuckle, reminding them of the first time they had flown. Papa Drake had been so proud, his webbed feet pattering on the bank as he encouraged them. Each one of them had wobbled and flapped, their wings still unsteady, but Papa Drake had believed in them, whispering words of encouragement with each clumsy attempt. "Remember, my little ones," he had said, his voice full of love, "You are meant to soar. Don't be afraid to spread your wings and fly."And they had flown, soaring high above the pond, the wind beneath their wings like a whispered promise. Now, as they watched the sun sink below the horizon, they thought of Papa Drake and the countless moments they had shared. He had taught them to swim, to dive for the tastiest fish, to build cozy nests with their own tiny beaks. He had shown them how to be kind, how to share, how to love with all their hearts. He had taught them, in his gentle way, how to be brave. Papa Drake had been their protector, their guide, their confidant. He had loved them unconditionally, and they had loved him in return, with a love that had no bounds. But Papa Drake was gone. The ducklings remembered the day he left, the deafening crack that had shattered the serenity of the pond, the sudden fear that had gripped their hearts. They remembered Mama Hen's frantic search, her worried cries echoing across the water.

They remembered the emptiness, the silence, the aching hole that had been ripped through their lives. And they remembered the love that had remained, a love that refused to be extinguished by the cruel hand of fate. Mama Hen, strong and resilient, had wrapped her wings around them, providing comfort and reassurance. She had spoken of Papa Drake, not with tears of grief, but with a gentle smile, sharing stories of his kindness, his courage, his unwavering love for them. She had taught them that even though Papa Drake was gone, his love still lived on in their hearts, in their memories, in every feather they found, in the whispers of the wind. Their lives had changed, but they were still a family, connected by an unbreakable bond of love and shared memories. They had learned to find joy in new experiences, to embrace the future with open wings. They had discovered that even in the face of loss, life went on, filled with beauty, laughter, and love. And they had found comfort in knowing that Papa Drake, in his own way, was still with them, guiding them, encouraging them, watching over them. Today, a rainbow arched across the sky, a vibrant tapestry of colors against the darkening canvas of the pond. The ducklings, nestled together, watched in awe. "Look!"whispered one duckling, his eyes wide with wonder. "It's a rainbow,"chirped another, his beak pointing towards the sky. "Papa Drake's rainbow,"added a third, his voice filled with a newfound understanding. Mama Hen, her heart swelling with love and pride, smiled down at her ducklings. She knew they were starting to understand, to heal, to accept. She gently nudged them closer, wrapping her wings around them, and spoke in a soft, reassuring voice. "Papa Drake is with us in every rainbow, in every sunrise, in every breeze that whispers his name. His love is always with us. And we will always remember him."The ducklings snuggled closer, their tiny hearts filled with warmth and comfort.

They knew, with a certainty that could not be shaken, that even though Papa Drake was gone, he was still with them. He was a part of them, woven into the fabric of their lives, his love a beacon guiding them through the darkness. They looked at each other, their eyes sparkling with hope. They had lost their Papa Drake, but they had gained a new understanding of life, a new appreciation for love, and a new strength that was born from the depths of their grief. They had learned to live with the ache of loss, to cherish the memories, to embrace the future. They had learned that love, like a rainbow, could bridge the gap between sadness and hope, between loss and life. As the rainbow faded, the ducklings, their hearts filled with a quiet peace, drifted off to sleep, their dreams filled with the gentle whispers of love and the vibrant colors of Papa Drake's rainbow. They knew, with absolute certainty, that Papa Drake was watching over them, his love a constant presence in their hearts, a guiding light on their journey through life. And they knew, with a growing sense of hope, that even though their world had changed, their love for each other and their memories of Papa Drake would always remain, a testament to the enduring power of family and the beauty of love that transcends even the boundaries of death.

Acknowledgements

Thank you to all the kindhearted friends and family who have supported me in this journey. Your encouragement and love have been a beacon of light throughout the writing process. I especially want to thank my parents whose insights and feedback have been invaluable.

Courtney resides in Georgetown, South Carolina with her husband and two children. Working on obtaining her law degree; Courtney put her love for writing on the back burner until recently, when she unexpectedly lost her brother; she then began devoting her time to create a story to help those like her and her family grieve their loss and in a way that children would be able to understand it.

When she is not writing, Courtney spends most of her time crafting, and enjoys reading snuggled up with her three dogs .